EXPLORING EARTH'S BIOMES

DESERT BIOMES
AROUND THE WORLD

by M. M. Eboch

Content consultant:
Rosanne W. Fortner
Professor Emeritus
The Ohio State University
Columbus, OH

CAPSTONE PRESS
a capstone imprint

Fact Finders Books are published by Capstone Press
1710 Roe Crest Drive, North Mankato, Minnesota 56003
www.capstonepub.com

Library of Congress Cataloging-in-Publication Data
Names: Eboch, M. M., author.
Title: Desert Biomes Around the World / by M. M. Eboch.
Description: North Mankato, Minnesota: Capstone Press, [2020] | Series:
  Fact Finders. Exploring Earth's Biomes | Includes index. | Audience: Age 8–9. |
  Audience: Grade 4 to 6.
Identifiers: LCCN 2019002052 | ISBN 9781543572032 (hardcover) | ISBN
  9781543575316 (paperback) | ISBN 9781543572155 (ebook pdf)
Subjects: LCSH: Desert ecology—Juvenile literature.
Classification: LCC QH541.5.D4 E26 2020 | DDC 577.54—dc23
LC record available at https://lccn.loc.gov/2019002052

Editorial Credits
Gina Kammer, editor; Julie Peters, designer; Morgan Walters, media researcher;
Kathy McColley, production specialist

Photo Credits
Alamy: Robert Fried, bottom right 8; Getty Images: FADEL SENNA, bottom 25;
National Geographic: John Kappler, 29; Newscom: Anthony Bannister/NHPA/
Photoshot, top right 15, OMAR KAMAL, VINCENT LEFAI AFP, middle 25;
Shutterstock: Andrei Rybachuk, 12, Anton Foltin, bottom 10, Aresium Images, spread
24-25, spread 26-27, spread 28-29, Arlene Waller, spread 14-15, spread 16-17, spread
18-19, spread 20-21, spread 22-23, Bildagentur Zoonar GmbH, bottom left 15, Charles
T. Peden, 16, 18, Danita Delmont, top 13, Elena11, bottom 4, Ernst Prettenthaler, bottom
6, Iryna Rasko, 20, Jonathan L Torres, background design element , Kekyalyaynen, 23,
Ken Wolter, 9, kojihirano, 17, lady-luck, (vector plants) Cover, loskutnikov, (sun) Cover,
LutsenkoLarissa, bottom 27, nashiihsan, 21, Oleg Gekman, (girl) Cover, Photonell_
DD2017, 14, Sergey Novikov, spread 4-5, spread 6-7, tntphototravis, top 11, Tom Roche,
spread 8-9, spread 10-11, spread 12-13, Tomasz Mazon, top 27, ventdusud, (valley)
Cover, Wojciech Dziadosz, bottom 7, Yusiki, top 5

TABLE OF CONTENTS

CHAPTER 1

HOT OR COLD BUT ALWAYS DRY

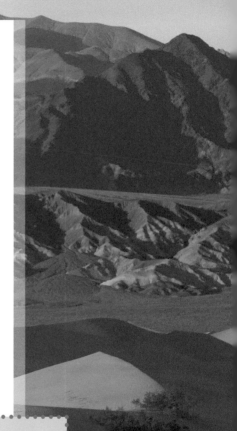

Picture a desert. Do you imagine something hot, dry, and empty? It's true that deserts are dry, but only some are hot. And deserts can be full of life.

Deserts are a type of biome. The other main biomes are forests, grasslands, tundra, and **aquatic**. Each type of biome has a particular type of **climate**. Each has animals and plants that can live there. Plants, animals, and people have all **adapted** to desert living. Some of those adaptations are wild!

FACT BOX
Earth isn't the only planet with deserts. Mars is cold and extremely dry. The entire planet is one big desert!

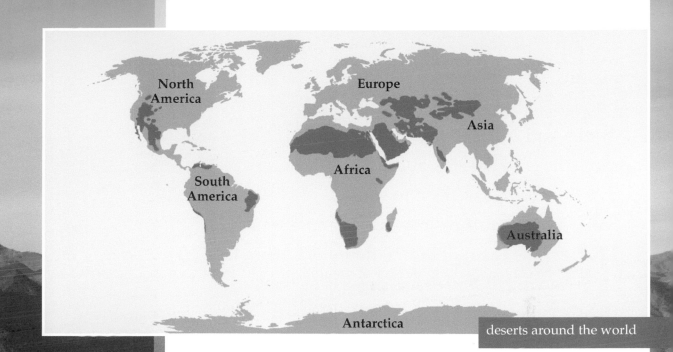

North
America

Europe

Asia

Africa

South
America

Australia

Antarctica

deserts around the world

WHAT MAKES A DESERT?

Deserts are found around the world. All these deserts share certain features. The most important is **precipitation**. A desert receives less than 10 inches (25 centimeters) of moisture each year. In the mainland United States, the average rainfall is about three times that.

The driest desert in the world is the Atacama Desert in Chile, South America. It only gets measurable rain every five to 20 years!

adapt—to change in order to survive; a change in an animal or plant to better fit its environment is called an adaptation
aquatic—having to do with water
climate—the usual weather conditions in a place
precipitation—moisture that lands on the ground, including rain, snow, hail, mist, or fog

5

Little rain means few clouds and plenty of sun. All that sun means many deserts are hot. Does the desert you pictured have sand dunes and camels? You may be thinking of the Sahara in Africa. About 2.5 million people live there, mostly close to sources of water. Sahara temperatures can rise to more than 122 degrees Fahrenheit (50 degrees Celsius).

The United States has deserts as well. Death Valley in California is the hottest place on Earth. Only a few hundred people live there. In one area, the average daily high in July and August is 115°F (46°C). Death Valley gets less than 3 inches (7.6 cm) of rain each year.

FACT BOX
The world's highest recorded temperature was in Death Valley: 134°F (56.7°C).

Death Valley in California

Antarctica is the coldest place on the planet. Huge windstorms pick up snow from the ground and turn into blizzards. Yet Antarctica gets very little precipitation. That makes it a desert—the largest one on Earth. The world's second-largest desert, the Arctic Desert, is also cold. This desert gets 6 to 10 inches (15 to 25 cm) of precipitation each year. Most of that falls as snow. Antarctica has no native populations, but the Arctic is home to 4 million people.

Deserts cover about one-fifth of Earth's surface. It's easier to live where water is plentiful. Still, deserts support a variety of life, including people.

desert in Antarctica

CHAPTER 2

LIVING THE DRY LIFE: PLANTS IN THE DESERT

Just as people need water to survive, so do plants. Desert plants have unique ways of getting water. They can also store water for long periods.

The cactus is perhaps the best-known desert plant. Cacti have spines instead of leaves. The spines don't lose moisture like leaves do. Spines may be long, stiff, and sharp, like large needles. Or they may look almost soft, like short, white hair. Some have hooked barbs on the ends. Spines make it harder for animals to eat the plants. It doesn't stop everyone, though. Prickly pears have flat pads covered in spines. Some people eat the pads like a vegetable. Countries such as Mexico, Italy, and South Africa grow cactus as a crop.

A man eats the pad of a prickly pear cactus.

Cactus flesh stores water. Mule deer, bighorn sheep, and jackrabbits know they can find water inside. Humans have learned this trick too. A hiker who gets lost in the desert might find water by cutting open a cactus. However, only certain types of cacti, such as a barrel cactus, contain drinkable water.

barrel cacti

FACT BOX

Some deserts have few plants of any kind. In polar deserts, most of the land is always covered by ice. The ice-free coasts hold almost all life.

About 2,000 different kinds of cacti exist around the world. They can look like barrels, blades of grass, pincushions, or even starfish. Firm, waxy skin holds in the water. Some cacti have very long but shallow roots. Saguaro cactus roots are typically 4 to 6 inches (10 to 15 cm) deep. Yet they can extend 50 feet (15 meters) to soak up hundreds of gallons of water from a light rain.

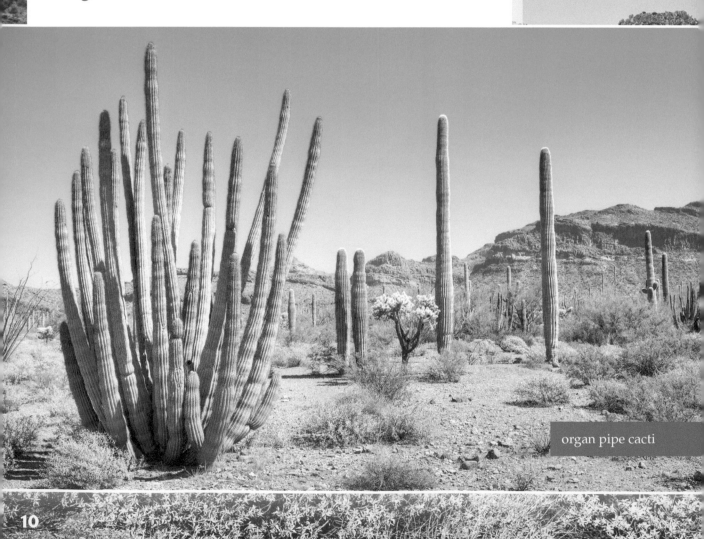

organ pipe cacti

A woodpecker and bee feed on the blooms of a Saguaro cactus.

Many cacti have bright flowers that become fruits full of seeds. Birds, bats, and insects feed on the flowers. Birds and animals eat the fruit and scatter the seeds. Wind and rain can also scatter seeds. A single cactus may produce millions of seeds. Only one or two will grow into a new cactus. Because they get little water, cacti grow slowly. Some, such as the Saguaro, may take a year to grow 1 inch (2.5 cm). Their slow growth rate means they need less water than most plants.

Aloe plants also have thick leaves that store water. The leaves are filled with a jellylike material. This gel stores water and energy for the plant. People use the gel to soothe burns and sunburns. Since the gel is mostly water, it adds moisture to burned skin. The substance that gives the plants energy helps heal human skin. For these uses, aloe plants are grown in dry areas around the world as crops.

aloe plants

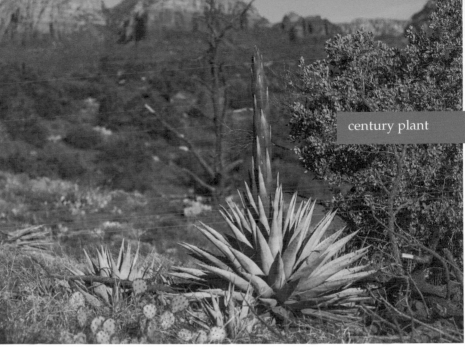

century plant

Century plants have a base of thick, swordlike leaves. From the middle, a tall, thin flower stalk rises up to 30 feet (9 m) high. Native Americans found many uses for the century plant. People can eat the base, stalk, seeds, and sap. The tough fibers can be woven into rope or rough cloth. Thorns on the leaves make good pins and needles.

FACT BOX

Century plants' leaves and roots foam when they are chopped and cooked. People have used this foam as soap.

CHAPTER 3

KEEPING COOL: ANIMAL ADAPTATIONS

If plants can survive in the desert, so can animals. They just need ways to handle the temperature, sun, and lack of water. Camels can go for weeks without eating or drinking. They have two rows of eyelashes to keep dust out of their eyes. They can even close their nostrils so they won't snort sand! These adaptations made camels perfect for carrying passengers with goods to trade across deserts.

Armadillo lizards live in the deserts of southern Africa. They hide in the cracks and crevices of large rocks. Their skin colors blend with the rocks, hiding them from **predators**. They eat desert plants and animals, such as scorpions. Meanwhile, birds of prey try to eat them. The frightened lizard puts its tail in its mouth and rolls into a ball. Then it's protected by its tough skin. The armadillo lizard can also drop its tail to escape.

An armadillo lizard curls up for protection.

thorny devil

In Australia, the thorny devil lizard has spikes all over its body. This protects it from predators. It gets moisture when dew settles on its skin. Grooves between its spikes draw the water toward the lizard's mouth.

predator—an animal that hunts other animals for food

Some desert animals come out only at night when it's cooler. Other animals are active only at dawn and at dusk. Those are the times to watch out for rattlesnakes! A few animals slow down when it's too hot or dry. The round-tailed ground squirrel sleeps through the summer. Desert toads sleep deep underground. They come out only when summer rains fill desert ponds.

ground squirrel

Some birds live in the desert only during certain seasons. They can fly long distances to find food or water. The tall Saguaro cacti offer a great view. Hawks perch on top to search for food over long distances. They may build nests of sticks between the cactus arms. Woodpeckers dig out nest cavities inside the cactus. If they stop using a nest, sparrows and other birds may move in.

A Harris's hawk perches on a Saguaro cactus.

Cacti provide the animals with food as well. Bats and insects get **nectar** and **pollen** from flowers. Many small animals eat the ripe fruit.

A ground squirrel eats the fruit of a prickly pear cactus.

Cacti even provide homes to animals such as the wood rat, also called the pack rat. These rats may build a den at the base of the cactus or use pieces of cacti in their dens. The cacti spines help protect the rats from predators such as foxes and coyotes.

Many animals have found ways to live in the desert. But climate change may make deserts even drier. Some animals then may struggle to survive.

FACT BOX

A pack rat family will use a den for generations. Some pack rat dens are more than 50,000 years old. Pack rats like to collect things, so their dens often hold ancient plants and bones. The pack rats' urine coats and preserves everything. Archaeologists study these dens to learn about the plants and animals of the past.

nectar—sweet liquid made by plants to attract insects and birds
pollen—a fine powder made by a flowering plant, needed to make new plants

CHAPTER 4

AT HOME IN THE HEAT: HUMANS IN DESERTS

People need water to survive. Deserts have few rivers, streams, or lakes. Yet people have lived in deserts for thousands of years. Many were **nomads**. They traveled to different places to find water and food each season. They typically hunted and harvested wild plants. Some raised animals adapted to desert living, such as camels.

Today over 1 billion people live in deserts. That's one-seventh of the world's population! But how do they manage the dry, hot climate?

People lead camels through the desert.

a camp in the Sahara Desert

People may dig wells to find water deep underground. They may also use **irrigation** to move water from wetter regions. In large deserts, people gather near oases. An oasis is a fertile piece of land around a fresh water supply. A few have enough water to support a village or a city. In the Sahara, two-thirds of the people live in oases. They use the water to grow fruit trees, vegetables, and grains.

Today trucks bring food grown other places to people in the desert. Air-conditioning keeps buildings cool. Modern irrigation methods can bring water from farther away.

irrigation—the act of supplying water to land in order to grow plants

nomad—a person who moves from place to place to find food and water, rather than living in one spot

In America, millions of people have moved to the Southwest. People like the region's warm temperatures and lack of rain. These benefits are also challenges. Desert cities must find ways to supply enough water. Some do water recycling to reuse **wastewater**. Wastewater can be used for irrigation or in factories. For these uses, the water doesn't have to be safe to drink. It takes more work to make water safe for drinking.

population change in the United States from July 1, 2017 to July 1, 2018

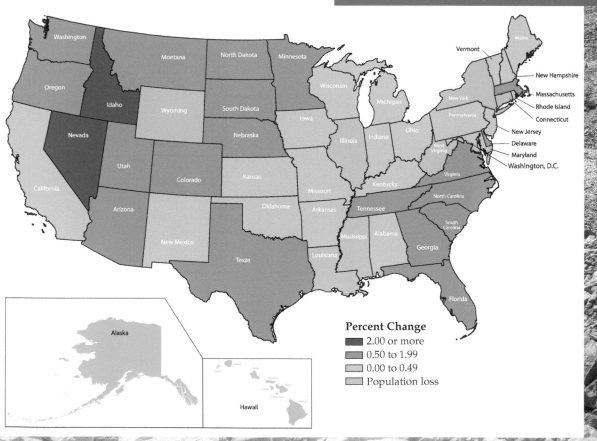

Percent Change
- 2.00 or more
- 0.50 to 1.99
- 0.00 to 0.49
- Population loss

Coastal areas can remove salt from seawater. Many countries in the Middle East and North Africa have large desalination facilities for this process. The United States also has some of these plants, mainly in California and Florida. However, the salt removal process is expensive.

People have come up with many ways to make desert living easier. Buildings are designed to use less water and keep people cool. Grassy lawns aren't a good idea in the desert. Instead, yards can have decorative rocks and plants that don't need much water.

FACT BOX

North America has four major deserts, all in the West. They are the Great Basin, Mojave, Sonoran, and Chihuahuan. This list doesn't include the part of the Arctic Desert that is in Alaska.

a water recycling sewage treatment station

wastewater—water that has been used by people

CHAPTER 5

DESERTS GROWING AND DYING

Deserts have a major **natural resource**—plenty of sun. That sunlight makes deserts ideal areas for **solar power**. Morocco has built a huge solar power plant in the Sahara. It looks like an ocean of reflective mirrors. Workers have to wear sunglasses to protect their eyes from the blinding glare. Thousands of mirrors direct the sun's rays to a tube. The sun heats a liquid in the tube. It produces steam, which powers an engine to make electricity. The site can provide electricity to more than 1 million people.

Deserts have other resources as well. Many are home to valuable metals such as gold, silver, and iron. Some deserts have large oil and natural gas deposits. These can be turned into electricity or fuel for vehicles.

Utah's Great Salt Lake Desert is a major source of sodium chloride. You probably know it by its common name, salt. The Great Salt Lake is very salty. Its water is left in shallow pools to **evaporate**. The salt left behind is then collected for cooking and other uses.

Noor solar power plant in Morocco

evaporate—to change from liquid into gas
natural resource—a material found in nature that people use, such as soil, air, trees, coal, and oil
solar power—energy from the sun that can be used for heating and electricity

Humans living in deserts have brought changes, including introducing invasive species. Native species are plants and animals that have lived in a place for centuries. They've adapted naturally over time. Invasive species are plants or animals that arrived recently. They may not have natural enemies. They can grow out of control and take over. If native species can't compete, they die out. This process can change and harm deserts and other biomes.

Sometimes invasive plants arrive by accident. Seeds are carried on shoes, by birds, or in the wind. People also introduce invasive species on purpose. The southwestern United States has changed hugely in the last two centuries. People brought livestock such as cows, which ate the desert grasses. This made room for invasive plants. People also planted invasive salt cedar trees because they liked how they looked. Salt cedar thrives in the desert's high heat and poor soil. The tree's deep roots drink any available water. They then release salt crystals that poison the ground and kill other plants.

salt cedar

Deserts are valuable, but that doesn't mean we want more of them. Yet some areas are turning into deserts. This process is called **desertification**. It may happen during a long **drought**. Cutting down trees can cause desertification. So can poor farming practices or using too much water for people and farms. Today climate change is turning more areas into deserts. Rivers dry up. Patterns of rain and snow change. Many plants die, and animals can't find food.

FACT BOX

As the planet warms, precipitation will increase. Scientists expect the Arctic to get less snow and much more rain. This change will hurt Arctic animals such as reindeer and polar bears.

People in Africa are trying to stop desertification around the Sahara. They are planting a 9-mile (14-km) -wide strand of plants that can resist drought. They hope to create a barrier to keep the desert from spreading. This "Great Green Wall" is 15 percent complete.

THE GREAT GREEN WALL INITIATIVE

MAURITANIA
MALI
NIGER
CHAD
SUDAN
ERITREA
DJIBOUTI
SENEGAL
BURKINA FASO
NIGERIA
ETHIOPIA

PARTICIPATING COUNTRIES

FOCUS AREA

The Great Green Wall goal is to stretch about 5,000 miles (8,000 km) from Djibouti to Senegal.

When the desert is damaged, it doesn't heal easily. Deserts must be managed well. Keeping cars on roads and trails is one way. It may mean keeping people out of some areas completely. With care, we can all keep enjoying deserts. They are important both to us and our planet.

FACT BOX

What can you do? Many cities use too much water. The water supply will eventually run out. People can help by using less water. Instead of planting a lawn, use decorative rocks and low-water native plants. This is a good practice everywhere, especially in the desert. You can search "conserve water" online for more ideas.

desertification—the process by which land becomes desert
drought—a long period of weather with little or no rain

GLOSSARY

adapt (uh-DAPT)—to change in order to survive; a change in an animal or plant to better fit its environment is called an adaptation

aquatic (uh-KWAH-tik)—having to do with water

climate (KLY-muht)—the usual weather conditions in a place

desertification (di-zur-tah-fah-KAY-shun)—the process by which land becomes desert

drought (DROUT)—a long period of weather with little or no rain

evaporate (i-VA-puh-rayt)—to change from liquid into gas

irrigation (ihr-uh-GAY-shun)—the act of supplying water to land in order to grow plants

natural resource (NACH-ur-uhl REE-sorss)—a material found in nature that people use, such as soil, air, trees, coal, and oil

nectar (NEK-tur)—sweet liquid made by plants to attract insects and birds

nomad (NOH-mad)—a person who moves from place to place to find food and water, rather than living in one spot

pollen (POL-uhn)—a fine powder made by a flowering plant, needed to make new plants

precipitation (pri-sip-ih-TAY-shun)—moisture that lands on the ground, including rain, snow, hail, mist, or fog

predator (PRED-uh-tur)—an animal that hunts other animals for food

solar power (SOH-lur POU-ur)—energy from the sun that can be used for heating and electricity

wastewater (WAYST-wah-tur)—water that has been used by people

READ MORE

Grady, Colin. *The Desert Biome.* Zoom in on Biomes.
New York: Enslow Publishing, 2017.

Perdew, Laura. *Deserts.* Landforms. Lake Elmo, MN:
Focus Readers, 2019.

Spilsbury, Louise, and Richard Spilsbury. *Desert Biomes.* Earth's
Natural Biomes. New York: Crabtree Publishing Company, 2018.

INTERNET SITES

DesertUSA
www.desertusa.com/

Exploring Extreme Environments: Deserts
http://extremeenvironmentsguide.weebly.com/deserts.html

World Biomes: Desert
http://kids.nceas.ucsb.edu/biomes/desert.html

CRITICAL THINKING QUESTIONS

1. Many desert animals are at risk. Should anything be done to protect them? How do you think people could help?
2. People use technology to make desert life easier. What is good about desert technology? What might be bad? Do you think technology will help in the future? Or will it do more harm than good?
3. Each year, many people move to deserts. They then need water for many uses. Should cities have to provide all the water people want? Should people have to use less water than they want? How should water use be managed?

INDEX